Leonard Bacon

Three Christmas Sermons

By the Sons of Leonard Bacon, Who Finished his Course Sunday,

December 25, 1881

Leonard Bacon

Three Christmas Sermons
By the Sons of Leonard Bacon, Who Finished his Course Sunday, December 25, 1881

ISBN/EAN: 9783744746373

Printed in Europe, USA, Canada, Australia, Japan

Cover: Foto ©Lupo / pixelio.de

More available books at **www.hansebooks.com**

THREE CHRISTMAS SERMONS

SUNDAY, DECEMBER 25, 1881.

BY SONS OF

LEONARD BACON

WHO FINISHED HIS COURSE

DECEMBER 24.

NEW HAVEN:

EDWARD P. JUDD.

1882.

Leonard Bacon.

IF we had limited ourselves to our original purpose, and printed this little book simply as a memorial gift to members of our family, no apology or explanation would have been needed.

Now that we have decided to offer to a wider circle of those who are bereaved in the departure of our father, these utterances of "the comfort wherewith we were comforted of God" on the sorrowful yet joyful Christmas-day just past, perhaps the exceptional character and circumstances of the book will still excuse us from any long preface.

These three sermons are printed as nearly as may be, in the form in which they were preached ; but the third, not having been originally written, has had to be reproduced from memory.

LEONARD WOOLSEY BACON,

Park Church, Norwich.

EDWARD WOOLSEY BACON,

First Church, New London.

THOMAS RUTHERFORD BACON,

Dwight Place Church, New Haven.

I.

THE FATHERHOOD FROM WHICH ALL FATHERHOODS ARE NAMED.

Preached to the Park Church, Norwich, Connecticut,

BY

LEONARD WOOLSEY BACON,

PASTOR.

THE FATHERHOOD FROM WHICH ALL FATHERHOODS ARE NAMED.

EPHESIANS, iii, 14. . . . THE FATHER FROM WHOM EVERY FAMILY [GR. FATHERHOOD] IN HEAVEN AND EARTH IS NAMED.

We need not grieve to miss, in the corrected translation of this text, the cherished phrase, "Father *of our Lord Jesus Christ*." There is no doubt what the meaning is; and if these very syllables are not in, the writing of Paul the Apostle himself, it is hardly less interesting and valuable to us to recognize in them the annotation of some of the earliest generations of those who believed through his word. In the next clause, if we seem to lose something in the absence of that phrase, "*the whole* family in heaven and earth," we gain more than we lose; for that which is named of God's fatherhood we find to be more even than the great fellowship of holy souls, the church in earth and heaven,—it includes all the families, lineages, fatherhoods (it

2

is a little difficult to find the exactly equivalent word) on earth, and whatever of the like may be carried over by us into the eternal life, or may subsist among the angels of God.

We cannot find it in our hearts to approach the words that speak to us of this holy mystery otherwise than with a most reverent and forbearing awe. Even if the vail of the temple is rent in twain, it is not for us to rush with audacious curiosity to gaze into "the holiest place of all." And when there comes near to us a messenger who has been privileged to see visions of things in heaven, and to hear words which it were not lawful for man to utter, and brings to us some word of knowledge that it hath well pleased the eternal One to make known to us, it is not for us inquisitively to cross-question him as if to extort from him more than it was given him to tell; but rather, with a reverential thankfulness, to receive the message in simplicity, content to know in part and prophesy in part, until that which is perfect be come, and the things that are in part shall be done away.

I do not need to tell you how far the church of Christ has seemed to come short of this grace of modesty and teachableness; how prone we have been to seize upon the word of the Lord as if it were only meant as a clue for our own speculative explorations into things unseen; or worse than this, as if the main use of it were to fortify us in our personal or partisan theories, and to furnish us weapons of offense against our fellow-Christians. Here in this text we have somewhat told us concerning fatherhood and sonship, such as might well have drawn all Christian hearts—all human hearts—together in brotherly love; but being received in the spirit of pride—pride of intellect, pride of sect—has been perverted into the occasion of whole libraries of barren speculation on questions known to no human mind, to fifteen centuries of acrimonious debate, and to the first great schism that tore the youthful church into two bleeding fragments.

It will help us to a better way of dealing with these cherished words, if we bear in mind that they contain *a revelation*—that they tell us something concerning the infinite and eternal God that we did not know and could not know of ourselves; something which might perhaps have been conjectured, doubtfully, but in which our conjectures were not unlikely to go amiss. And so, in fact, we find, as soon as we begin to read the words with simplicity, that our conjectures had really inverted the order of the truth and put that first which is last. All earthly father-hoods are named from the Fatherhood of God. Have we not been in the habit of thinking, you and I, that it was just the other way—that our Father who is in heaven was so called from a certain analogy with our fathers who are in earth—that the earthly fatherhoods are the re-ality, and the divine Fatherhood a figure of speech?—that this calling of God "Our Father," arises out of our habit of thinking, by which we impute to him the acts and qualities of a human parent?—that there is no real Fatherhood in God, independently of our habits of conceiving and expressing? Is not this something like what has been in your thoughts and mine?

And now, as if to show how high, like the heaven above the earth, are God's thoughts above our thoughts, we have this revelation of an eternal reality. We learn that this Father-hood of God is something more than a mode of our thinking, derived from our study of earthly things, varying with human moods, vanishing in human darkness or unbelief. It is something as real, as eternal, as God himself. It is in him, not in us. You may tell me that the word is of recent use—that the elder world had not learned to say Our Father, but only Our King, and that this gentler word came in in gentler days, the days of the gospel; and what you thus say will be partly true and partly false; but false. or true, it does not affect the everlasting truth of God's Fatherhood. That is "forever settled in the heavens," even though all the earth were blind to it. Even if men to-day could unlearn the dear lesson Christ has taught us; and wholly stifle that inward whisper that prompts to say Abba, Father; and if the little children of the age to come could grow up in terror of God, not knowing, or not daring, to say "Our Father who art in heaven;" and the nations having lost their light should begin to say of God, what some seem trying so persistently to teach themselves to say, "he is a cruel Destiny—he is an unpity-ing, unrelenting system of natural laws—he is a passionless nucleus of abstract infinitudes"—this could not change the everlasting truth. The

fatherly heart of God, which pitieth us as a
father pitieth his children, would go beating on,
and measuring with its great pulsations of love
the eternity to come, like as it has the eternity of
old, in the beginning or ever the earth was.
This is the teaching of the text—that, perhaps,
which the theologians of the early church meant
to set forth in the ancient creeds under the
phrase "the eternal generation"—that God was
always the Father, that his paternity is that
which "was in the beginning, is now, and ever
shall be, world without end;" and that it is after
this eternal type of fatherhood subsisting in God
before all worlds, that every family—all fatherhood—in heaven and earth is constituted and
named. O parents, who, as the year ripens to
the Christmas-tide, love to give good gifts to
your children, are happy at the thought of their
coming gladness, and glow with a pure delight
at the response of their loving gratitude, know
that this fairest, most unselfish thing in human
nature is in you because it was first in God; a
lineament, not yet destroyed, of that fair image
of himself in which he created man. It is even
thus, as ye love to give good gifts to your

children, that he "loveth to give the Holy Spirit to them that ask him."

And this eternal and infinite fact it is, of the Fatherhood of God, in its highest manifestation toward Jesus Christ the Son, that is drawing the special thoughts of the church in every land at this Christmas season. Its highest manifestation, I say, not its only one. There be many sons of God; for he, the Former of our bodies, is the Father of our spirits. Even the heathen poet sang, "for we are also his offspring;" and the apostle to the heathen caught from those Gentile lips the word, and sent it back to his pagan hearers stamped with a divine endorsement—"Forasmuch, then, as ye are the offspring of God." The apostasy of the human race from God has not sufficed to rupture the bonds that hold them members of his family. He grieves over them in their far-off absence, saying, "How can I give you up?" And if they will but arise and go to him, he meets them a great way off, and kisses them, and rejoices more over the wanderer returned than over him that was ever with him. O, sinful man, conscious of persistent sin, God is your Father and he loves you.

And in spite of all you are, you are his children, yet you love him not.

But there is a higher sense, in which this expression of God's Fatherhood is used in special relation to *good* men—men who mean to do good and try to do good from day to day—men who trust in God—believers—who serve God—who love God. These are his sons. They have received power — privilege — the right — to *become* sons of God. They are doubly his—by nature and by patent of adoption. The family likeness comes out in them. They share the family aims and counsels, and their Father's will is their will. They do not serve by constraint, but by love. There is only one interest in the family, for the Father's kingdom and estate is theirs, and what is done for him is done for themselves. The family instinct is strong within them, and grows stronger every day. There is that in their hearts that moves them to say Father—Abba, Father. It is the adopting Spirit, and by this it is that they know that they are sons of God, and if children then heirs—heirs of God and joint heirs with Jesus Christ. There is something of the just family

pride that belongs to them, too. A right noble
name is this which they bear about in the
world, that they should be called sons of God.
And the thought of it lifts up their souls above
the power of mean temptations, and makes
lowly and humble ones to be kings and priests
like their royal Father. Do not, O believers,
shrink from the wearing of that magnificent
title which he hath with his own hand conferred
upon you. Beloved, now are you a son of God.
And it doth not yet appear what you shall be.
This only we know—these distortions and mar-
rings of your Father's likeness in you that make
you seem to others, and to yourself sometimes,
a sort of caricature of the family likeness, will
fade out as you know your Father better, and
by and by they will wholly disappear, and you
shall be like him when you see him as he is.

But even this is not God's highest Fatherhood.
There is an eternal love which is the type after
which not only all loving relationships of earth
are fashioned, but whatever in heavenly worlds
there may be of like links and chains of personal affection. And to know something of this
deep wonder of love in the heart of God, we

turn to-day to contemplate the manger in which there lies a little speechless infant wrapped in swaddling clothes, concerning whom, among all the sons of God, it is testified from heaven that he is *the* Son of God; and among those who are begotten of God to a living hope, that he is the *only* begotten of the Father; and among us who have such abounding tokens of God's infinite fatherly love toward us, it is declared (as if there were no other) that he is "God's dear Son," his "well beloved Son, in whom he is well pleased."

What great deeps of mystery are touched and bordered by these words, I do not know. They know least in such a matter who are sure they know it all—that they have "found out the Almighty to perfection;" and they are wisest who are most deeply conscious how much there is they cannot understand. I study to content myself with a very little knowledge that is much like not knowing; and to be well assured that what I do know, I *know*. Out of all the variances of good men in the study of the Scriptures, the very least that we can claim as settled beyond all dispute is this, that Jesus Christ is Son of God in a unique sense of the word, such as does not suffer us to class him as one of the sons of God. He, the Son, reveals the Father; "neither knoweth any man the Father, save the Son, and he to whom the Son will reveal him." How can one know the Fatherhood but by knowing the Sonship?

We, then, longing to know more of the Father from whom we have wandered and lost ourselves, turn this day to look towards the manger where the young child lies. The heaven seems to bend over him with joy and greeting. A loving Providence protects him. The grace of God is upon him. He delights to do God's will, and wonders that they do not understand that he must be at his Father's house and about his Father's business. As he grows older, he "grows in favor with God." And when at last, come to manhood, he longs to fulfil all righteousness and draws near to John to be baptized, the voice of God declares, "This is my beloved Son, in whom I am well pleased." He lives on every word proceeding from the mouth of God, esteeming it more than necessary food. And after long days of toil, sleep is not so sweet to him as to spend the night alone on the mountain-top with the Father. And when the Father seems to have left him alone in his last distress, it breaks his heart; he cries out, "My God, my God, why hast thou forsaken me?" and dies. But the eternal answering love, that must needs be hidden from the dying Son, was there. The clouds and darkness that are round about the throne of God part here and there a moment, and through the rifts we get a strange, awful glimpse as if of anguish on the face of God blessed forever. It is the demonstration how great was his love for us, that he spared not his own Son from agony and death, but delivered him up for us all. He was so well beloved a Son; in him the Father was so well pleased, that the love which spared him not must have been love indeed!

If we wholly knew the heart of God, we should, in the light of this text, have great advantage in understanding these earthly fatherhoods that are "named therefrom." If we knew familiarly the imperial features of Alexander the Great, how easily we could judge of his likeness on any coin of his reign! But now we have to judge the emperor from the coin, not the coin from the emperor. The best we can do is to sort over the shining hoard of the antiquary, and cull the best impressions, the least worn and defaced with the sordid uses of the world, and judge the original by comparing these among themselves. We are not in a position to reason downward from God to men; we must reason upward from the things which are seen to that which is unseen; we must know the original type by collating the least imperfect copies.

If it has been given to you to know through all your years of life an example of long-sustained unwavering fatherly affection that was made up of inseparable love and righteousness, an example in which the noblest elements in human nature, still more ennobled by the grace of God, came most manifestly near to the divine likeness, in which shone out upon you, as steadfast as "the patient stars," an undiscourageable hopefulness that resolutely would foresee in you a better end beneath all unpromising traits of character, an infinite, surprising patience with immaturities and weaknesses and the faults of a less magnanimous nature than his own, a simple-minded forgetfulness of his own great deeds in his affectionate delight in any worthy act well done on the part of any of his children, as if he loved to look down from the unconscious height of his great fame and say, "this is my beloved son in whom I am well pleased,"—then you can not be far amiss in saying, Herein I see something of what that fatherly heart of God must be from whom all earthly fatherhoods are fashioned and named.

If it has been given you to see the bravest heart you ever knew—so unselfish, so heroic, whom no personal danger could make afraid, from whose firm lips no extremity of anguish of his own could extort one complaint, groaning in spirit as he said, "there is no sorrow in life like the sorrow of losing a grown-up son," bowing with unutterable tenderness in the agony of parting with the fairest, noblest, saintliest of his sons, yet singing with a loud voice of triumph beside his grave,—you would be tempted to say to yourself, I cannot understand the mystery of godliness, into which the angels desire to gaze, how God spared not his own Son but freely gave him up for us all, and yet gave him as the last proof of love, and as if there had been some divine anguish in the sacrifice—I cannot understand it; but this fatherhood on earth which is named of God the Father is given me that I might learn God therefrom; and even now in part I see, and in part I prophesy." And if you should be tempted thus to speak, you could not be very greatly wrong.

And if the glow of a true answering love and gratitude has ever burned within your heart; if, waking from the unconsciousness of childhood that took all daily helps and comforts as a matter of course, you have come to know what long, unselfish toil and care they stood for; if you have learned to trace the very thoughts of your mind to the quickening suggestions of his great intellect, your worthiest plans and achievements to the germs of his planting; if you have been wont to count that the best hours of your life were those spent in his companionship, and that his approval and good pleasure were your best reward for good work well done, and your strong incentive for working on to make the world happier and better even as "your father worketh hitherto;" then you may take these holy thoughts and experiences with you to the sacred pages of the New Testament of our Lord and Saviour Jesus Christ, feeling that you have learned the elements of that human language in which the book is written; that the mystery of godliness, without controversy great, is not all a mystery; that you have come in some wise to know the Son from whom all filiations in heaven and earth are named; and that when "Jesus lifteth up his eyes to heaven and saith, Father," and when the voice from heaven answers, "My beloved Son," you are not wholly a stranger in the family.

You have heard, my dear friends, that only a few hours ago my dear and honored father, known, loved, praised in the gospel throughout all the churches, ceased suddenly from his blessed labors, and entered into his blessed rest. You will not wonder or complain that, this happy Lord's day, when "the voice of rejoicing and salvation is in the dwellings of the righteous," my thoughts should turn from the story of the young child wrapped in swaddling-clothes and lying in a manger, to the dear old man wrapped in his grave-clothes and resting sweetly on his bier, and should find in this lesson of my father's

holy life and death some light on the eternal
Fatherhood of Him who is the God and Father
of our Lord Jesus Christ, and our Father, and
our God.

•

II.

GOD NEVER OLD.

Preached to the First Church of Christ in New London, Connecticut,

BY

EDWARD WOOLSEY BACON,

PASTOR.

GOD NEVER OLD.

LUKE II, 40.--AND THE CHILD GREW AND WAXED STRONG, FILLED WITH WISDOM: AND THE GRACE OF GOD WAS UPON HIM.

Not least among the attractions of our blessed faith is the youthfulness in which it has pleased God to express his revelation. The incarnation of God comes to us as an infant; and, if the years grow old and roll away into the past, if life grows weary and passes out of youth, if death invades the earthly home and breaks it up and its associations hurry toward oblivion,—however we are reminded of decay, the star of Bethlehem invites us to rejoice in a God ever living, who delights in youth and chooses to become manifest to the world through infancy. His is "the power of an endless life," and, when we remember his advent in human form, we do well to gather around us these symbols from the forest, that grow richer the colder the climate and the

deeper the snow, and are green as long as they
live.

Perhaps such thought of God is hardly natural; but it is just. He never grows old, and the
Scriptures are careful to teach us his perennial
vigor. "From everlasting to everlasting he is
God;" but "a thousand years are with him as
one day."

Think of it:

> Hast thou not known? Hast thou not heard
> That the everlasting God, the Lord,
> The Creator of the ends of the earth,
> Fainteth not, neither is weary?
> There is no searching of his understanding.
> He giveth power to the faint;
> And to them that have no might he increaseth strength.
> Even the youths shall faint and be weary,
> And the young men shall utterly fail:
> But they that wait upon the Lord shall renew
>   their strength:
> They shall mount up with wings as eagles:
> They shall run and not be weary;
> They shall walk and not faint.

That is the Scriptural idea of God always, and
especially in those prophecies that are most full
of anticipation of the manifestation of God's

glory in the face of Jesus Christ. And not the least that we learn from Christ is this revelation of the youthfulness of God. When we would see God, we are taken first of all, not to the Temple, not to the Rabbis, not to the worker of miracles, but to Bethlehem, to the manger; and this is the sign to us: "we find a babe, wrapped in swaddling clothes, and lying in a manger."

The same demonstration of what (for want of easier phrase) I must poorly call the youthfulness of God, is taught to the very end of Christ's ministry. He did not remain an infant, although he appeared in the freshness of infancy. Of course the child grew and waxed strong. Naturally he became filled with wisdom, and the spirit of God was upon him. But he did not grow old; he grew only to the prime of life; he was young at his death; he was but thirty-three years old. Have you ever observed how full of young life the gospels are? The aged Zacharias, the aged Simeon, the aged Anna, are at the beginning; but they salute the blessed infancy and "depart in peace, having seen the salvation of God." And after these early chapters of Luke, where do you read of old age again, except

in the subjects of Jesus' healing who, waiting
upon him, renewed their strength? If we turn
far over into the Epistles, we come into contact
with men old enough; with " such an one as Paul
the aged," now "ready to be offered, the time of
whose departure is at hand;" and read the sad-
dening expressions of Peter, as he says with the
solemnity of age, " I think it right, as long as I
am in this tabernacle, to stir you up by putting
you in remembrance; knowing that the putting
off of my tabernacle cometh swiftly; . . . . that
you may be able, after my decease, to call these
things to remembrance."

But turn back to the Gospels and you are
again in quite a different company. There is no
feebleness here; these are no old man's halting
counsels that we read from His lips " who spake
as never man spake." He gathered young men
about him and made them his apostles; and the
story of his teaching, his athletic itineracy, his
endurance—continuing all night in prayer,—his
longing for a home which he could not have,
his fondness for little children, his love for the
rich young man, his zealous purification of the
Temple, his very appearance, which caused his

opponents to allege his youth against his wisdom;—all these and many other features of the gospels create for us, as we read, a very atmosphere of young maturity that is no small element of the power of their story.

Nor does their youthful character make the gospels only helpful to the young; it, rather, heightens their attractiveness to the aged and infirm. For a healthful and good old age is ever green in spirit and loves to refresh itself by intercourse with youthful vigor. It is a mistaken kindness which undertakes to "get the old people together," thinking to make them enjoy themselves; the greatest satisfaction that age can have is in the society of the young and strong. The gospels are, primarily, books for the young; but, by that very fact, they are books for the aged too.

I have put the Epistles as expressing age, in contrast with the gospels, that tell the story of the life of Jesus. But, whenever the Epistles refer to Christ, it is always with this decided impression of his youth. Down to their latest day, he remained, to the companions of his ministry, the same young man that he was

in Capernaum, in Pilate's judgment-hall, at Calvary and on the Mount of Olives, when "he was
parted from them and a cloud received him out
of their sight." I do not mean that their Lord
became no more to them than a memory of
youthful intimacy: I could not say that. They
have much to declare of his exaltation, his
glory, his majesty; but there is no change in
the impression of his youth; it is eternal; it has
"the power of an endless life." Even the phrase
"our elder brother," by which we so often describe Christ, is not a scriptural expression.
He is our brother and "made like unto his
brethren in all things;"—it is most natural for
us to call him "elder brother;" but, his vigor-
ous youth was so indelibly stamped upon their
minds, the apostles never speak of him as older
than themselves were in their youth;—much less
do they describe him as "old." Even Paul, who
never saw Jesus in the flesh, but to whom he
became manifest in a vision, partakes of this
same unconscious recognition of his Lord as
young. And when we reach the very end, in the
vision of the Revelation, what is the imagery of
the poem when it tells of the consummation of

Christ's glory and his final triumph in his kingdom, but of the church as the young bride,
adorned for her youthful husband?

It was, then, not without purpose that, "when
the fulness of time came, God sent forth his Son,
born of a virgin." It was that when we would
see God we should return from weariness and
from sin as if renewing our life, as if becoming
pure in heart, and behold him first of all in a
Babe, wrapped in swaddling clothes and lying
in a manger!

It was not without purpose that "the child
grew and waxed strong, filled with wisdom; and
that the grace of God was upon him." It was
that we, drawing near to him and becoming as
babes in Christ, might grow in mind and spirit,
as he grew in favor with God and men.

And it was not without purpose that, in the
prime of life, at the very opening of manhood,

"He was taken from prison and from judgment:
 And who shall declare his generation?
 For he was cut off out of the land of the living!"

It was that he should stand before men forever the exponent of the youthfulness of "the

everlasting God, who fainteth not, neither is weary."

When he came to earth it was in the exquisite simplicity of infancy; that henceforth every cradle might speak of God to us; and when he rose from the grave, because he could not be holden of death, and ascended upon high, it was in the likeness of perfect manhood, at its young maturity, that we might think of him as young forever; and of God as imaged by him; and of those who are with him where he is, as touching the hem of his garment, healed of their infirmities, restored to a perennial youth. Time drew no lines upon his brow, nor were his shoulders bent by weight of years; and they that sleep in him shall God bring with him, the wrinkles smoothed away and the outward form, no longer a temporary tabernacle, but an eternal house,—made as youthful as the cheerful spirit that waited upon him, as youthful as he is! No one can be in sympathy with Christ and not become like Him; and he who "humbled himself to be born of a virgin," and who as a child "grew and waxed strong and became filled with wisdom," never grew old, even in the powers of the body; he is young forever. He manifests in the flesh, "The everlasting God, that fainteth not, neither is weary."

This is one of the lessons that grow out of the remembrance of how "Jesus was born in Bethlehem of Judea in the days of Herod the king," and of how "the child grew and waxed strong."

In how many villages, in how many homes, are those common chronicles made: "She brought forth her first born son"—"The child grew and waxed strong." In how many homes is the chronicle added of pining sickness, feeble maturity, trembling old age, or sudden death! Thus has it been, thus it is to-day to some of us. It is a merry day; but not where Christmas letters lie unopened or where Christmas gifts are held unsent. And yet it should be a glad day even in such homes; and it is, in some such homes by these tokens of which I have reminded you so feebly. O that wherever there is sorrow, wherever there is foreboding, wherever the end of the months seems sad, and the indications of decay stand out,

"Before the music of the year
Its varied notes shall cease,

> May Christmas raise a melody
> Of happiness and peace.
> And when the solemn final chord
> Has died upon the ear,
> May strains of gladness, full and free,
> Awake the coming year!"

To one who understands what the birth of Jesus is, or what is the meaning of the Star of Bethlehem, the joy of this day is different from any other gladness, and so profound that no shock of earth can ruffle it; else why should I,—how could I be preaching to you to-day?

I pray God you may take the birth of Jesus in its true significance!

Its significance is this, to young and old: "Beloved, now are we children of God, and it is not yet made manifest what we shall be. But we know that when he shall be manifested, we shall be like him; for we shall see him, even as he is!"

III.

EMMANUEL—GOD WITH US.

Preached to the Dwight Place Church, New Haven,
Connecticut,

BY

THOMAS RUTHERFORD BACON,

PASTOR.

EMMANUEL—GOD WITH US.

MAT. I, 23.—AND THEY SHALL CALL HIS NAME EMMANUEL, WHICH BEING INTERPRETED IS, GOD WITH US.

This is the day upon which the Christian world has declaredly or tacitly agreed to commemorate a great historical event. We need not now enter upon a discussion of the reasons which led to the setting apart of this particular day for this purpose. The fact is, for our present use, sufficient, that to-day men everywhere remember with joy that Jesus was born in Bethlehem of Judea. We keep the feast with gladness, with praise to God on our lips and in our hearts, with the interchange of tokens of sweet domestic and friendly affection, with remembrance of the poor, whom we have always with us, with every effort to make the earth brighter with the love of man and the glory of God. And this is fitting, for we celebrate thus the day which brought glory to God in the highest, and peace on earth, good will to men. For then God was found in the likeness

4

of men, that men might be found in the likeness
of God; the divine was made human to teach us
how the human might be made divine; the Son
of God became the son of man, that we the deso-
late children of men might be given power to
become the sons of God; God was manifest
in the flesh that man might be manifest in the
Spirit. Therefore keep the day with "solemn
mirth" and gladness, rejoicing in the goodness
of the Lord for his unspeakable gift. "For-he
who spared not his own Son but delivered him
up for us all, how shall he not with him also
freely give us all things?"

And yet a question may properly arise which
cannot but give a very sober turn to our thought
to-day. Why should we rejoice in the birth of a
child? Born in labor and pain, living in joy
which is so checkered with sorrow that oftenest
the sorrow is greater than the joy, and going out
at last in dreadful, mysterious death, what is
man, that any one should rejoice that another
human life is begun? And in this particular
case of which we now speak, how little there is
from the material point of view, that could
give occasion for joy to any prophetic soul who

could look forward over the earthly life of this little child. The babe now wrapped in swaddling clothes and lying in a manger should be despised' and rejected of men, a man of sorrows and acquainted with grief. His brief years should be spent in labor and pain, and, in the full promise of his gifted manhood, he should be crushed to death by an awful catastrophe to which· no touch of agony or shame was wanting. "The overture of the angels" was the bright prelude to the darkest of all earthly tragedies. But in that choral joy no minor strain of sadness was blended to prophesy the sorrow which was to come. The star which led the patient watchers of the skies from their far eastern home, shone fair and bright, undimmed by the coming darkness of Calvary. Why, at the beginning of this sad career, was there joy in the presence of the angels, and why did these shining messengers of God hasten to proclaim this birth as glad tidings of great joy to the lowliest shepherds of Bethlehem? Why did the heavens by their unwonted splendor declare the promise of God's glory, when this man was born of woman, whose days should be full of labor and sorrow? It was only because his name should be called Emmanuel which is by interpretation, God with us.

Because the incorruptible Spirit of God dwelt in that corruptible clay and the power of an endless life strengthened the weakness of that mortal being, therefore " the morning stars sang together and all the sons of God shouted for joy." They saw then, as we see now, that God was with us and that the miseries of earthly existence should only serve to manifest the glory of this eternal life. Violence, wrath, insult, death, should fall upon him, and their blows should break the alabaster box and there should flow forth ointment of spikenard, very precious, to fill the earth with a divine perfume. We see that this was an occasion for unmingled joy, for the babe born in Bethlehem waxed strong, and as he met the enemies of man's joy he destroyed them ; and overcame the last enemy, even death. Temptation, suffering, destruction, at the touch of his creative Spirit were transfigured and became the means of glory and eternal peace. Doing his Father's will, fulfilling all righteousness, by the things which are seen and are temporal, he was lifted to the things which are unseen and are eternal. The divine life which thrilled his soul made earthly sorrows the stepping-stones to immortal joys. Because his name was Emmanuel, he rose above these mortal griefs to the eternal glory of the blessedness of God. Before that infinite blessedness, the pain of Gethsemane and Calvary become as nothing; or rather give to it its brightest splendor, its most poignant joy. Shine on, undimmed, O star of Bethlehem, for "the people that sat in darkness have seen a great light!" Shout aloud in your joy, ye multitude of the heavenly host, for "the tabernacle of God is with men!" The name of the child is called Emmanuel.

And this same fact which justified the rejoicings over the birth at Bethlehem, makes the joy which hails the birth of any child reasonable. The world-old instinct of the human heart, which compels it to an unreasoning joy when a new soul comes into being, has seemed to some men mistaken and untrue. And looked at in the light of the personal history of most of the sons of men and with no light from heaven to explain its correspondence with the purpose and work of God, it is perfectly unreasonable. Most lives, from a material point of view, are the merest wrecks. From the drift-wood of these wrecks the coming generations may build homes for themselves, but in the matter of personal conscious existence, the lives of men are full of labor and pain, prematurely ended, or stretching out their years through slow decay, until destruction claims them as its own. From such a point of view no life is really worth living to him who lives it. It may serve some ends in the advancement of the race, but so far as the man himself is concerned, it were better that he had not been. Therefore this instinct of the race is not only unreasoning but unreasonable. The joy of the mother in all her pain, because her child is born, is a valuable mechanical accident, (I had almost said—contrivance) for the perpetuation of the species for some doubtful end, but is not justified by any philosophical view of the circumstances. But if, of all the unnumbered millions of children who have been born, one is rightly called Emmanuel, then the mother's joy is right, and we learn that the sweet domestic instincts are true, the exponents of the wise, loving, eternal purpose of God. For if

God be with us, who can be against us. The
swaddling clothes and the manger, the sign declared by the angel of the Lord, were a sign not
only of one who should rise above the sorrows
of earth to the glory of heaven, but of Christ,
the Lord, a Saviour, born unto us, who should
lift the children of sorrow into the joy of the
sons of God. Being joined to him by faith we
rise above and beyond the grief and misery of
earth, knowing that our citizenship is in heaven,
where Christ is at the right hand of God. For
we have here no continuing city, but we seek
one to come. If for us his name is not Emmanuel, then are we wretched indeed, but if he really
is *God with us*, the power of his endless life is in
us, and now are we the sons of God. Herein we
know that the domestic instincts are part of the
impress of that image in which we were created,
and thrill in unison with the pulsations of the
eternal heart of God, and that the celestial, unreasoning joy of motherhood, upon which none
but modern materialism has ever dared to lay a
sacrilegious hand, is justified, because it is in con-
sonance with the reasonable hope that the life
begun may come to rest upon the child who was

called Emmanuel, and thus may rise above the sins and sorrows and immaturities of earth into the holy and eternal perfection of the kingdom which is righteousness and peace and joy in the Holy Ghost. For whoso finds God with him shall prevail over temptation, pain, and death, and life's darkest tragedy shall become bright and beautiful as the glory of the Lord shines round about him.

My brethren, dearly beloved, yesterday morning, as you have heard, just before the light of a new day broke in the east, my venerable and honored father passed away from earth. I should not venture to intrude my personal grief upon the bright joy of your Christmas morning, did I not know that this loss of mine is your loss also, and that the cloud that rests above my home to-day, casts its shadow over many of the homes of this people. And my thought goes out, and my words must lead your thought to the stable of Bethlehem, in the ancient and storied East, where a young mother rejoiced over her first-born son, and to a little cabin in the new and pathless West, where also a young mother rejoiced that her first-born son was come into the world, now almost eighty years ago. If the gladness of the one was an echo of the joy of God and his angels, not less truly so was the gladness of the other. For the little child of Bethlehem took this little child of the wilderness by the hand, and led him in the way everlasting. This new mortal life was touched by the power of an endless life and became immortal, drawing its vital energy from the source of eternal being. And the child grew and waxed strong in spirit, and the grace of God was upon him, for he learned to call his God, Emmanuel. You mourn with me to-day, and all the city shares my grief, not because of the great natural powers and faculties with which he was endowed, but because of the moral force which sanctified those powers and faculties for the help of man; because God added to these other gifts the unspeakable gift of his grace in Christ, which made him great. O the services which he has rendered to this community as a minister of righteousness in that ancient church which is the mother of us all; as a citizen who found no political duty of slight importance; as a man whose immeasurable love was directed by a clear common sense; who

could never see a wrong thing without earnestly
laboring to set it right; who could never see an
opportunity of helping men without seeking to
improve it to the uttermost—of his public services to this community and to the world, I do
not need to speak to you who have felt the bene-
ficent influence of his life. He rests from his
labors and his works do follow him. Nor can I
trust myself to speak of those wonderful traits
of character which made him the contemporary
and the dear companion of all his children, of
the youngest, no less than of the eldest. For the
most remarkable side of his remarkable life was
wholly hidden from the world and was found in
the circle of his domestic affections, where the
beauty of Godlike holiness shone out upon
those whom God had given him, and kept his soul
in perpetual youth, to sympathize with the work
and aims of his children and his children's
children. While every revelation of God was
dear to him, perhaps that which was dearest, cer-
tainly that to which he oftenest referred in his
home, was the revelation of the God of the family,
the covenant God, whose mercy is from everlasting to everlasting upon them that fear him, and

nis righteousness unto children's children, to such as keep his covenant and remember his commandments to do them. And the promise of the Lord standeth sure. It is enough for me now to say that his greatness was of that rare kind which seems greatest to those who knew him best. Few words are fittest; he has fought a good fight, he has finished his course, he has kept the faith, he has received the crown. Nothing is left to mortal sight save the earthly house of the tabernacle wherein he dwelt, which shall shortly be committed to the ground; earth to earth, ashes to ashes, dust to dust. And we shall see his face no more.

Brethren, does my Christmas greeting seem to you a sombre, and even a sorrowful one? It is not so. The greeting may be solemn, but it is not sad. Behind the natural tears for my own great loss, behind the tremor of the voice of one from whom a great part of the interest of this earthly life is gone, there is a deep, an infinite, a triumphant joy which nothing can take from me. For the life now ended in a peaceful death was so complete and so splendid in the grace of him who is called Emmanuel, that it testifies to me beyond a doubt that God is with us. Living, he lived unto the Lord; dying, he died unto the Lord; living and dying he was the Lord's.

Standing by that beloved form in which he had tabernacled for almost eighty years, in the dawning light of yesterday, I knew—I felt in my inmost soul—that the clay upon which I looked was not he. Beautiful as it was with all the glory of gray-haired age, I knew it was but the house from which the tenant was gone, and that he was with God in the spirit who had been with him in the flesh. And in that hour I knew that I must speak to you to-day, and must bring to you a Christmas greeting of joy. And by his complete and righteous life, the greeting comes from him and not from me. He being dead, yet speaketh, however feebly, through my unworthy lips. And the message which I bring to you from that cold form, upon this bright Christmasday, is this: The name of the child, who was born in Bethlehem of Judea in the days of Herod, the King, is called Emmanuel.

And I bring this message from one who found God with him here and who has now gone to be with God in glory everlasting. By the power of the present God he lived for the help of man, in the faith of the present God he died to enter into the glory of the Lord. God was with him and God is with us.

O, my brethren, if Jesus is not known to you by the name Emmanuel; if he seems only as a mythic, or at most an historic, figure, far removed from our present needs and distresses, if God is to you only a God afar off and not a God nigh at hand, accept the testimony of the life just ended, which bears witness, like that of John, that the Son of Thunder may be the disciple whom Jesus loves, and who rests upon his bosom; and learn that the faith of Christ can give an unmeasured moral power to the feeble child of poverty and want who finds his portion in the service of his God. As I stood by that death-bed and remembered the aspiration of the prophet, "Let me die the death of the righteous, and let my last end be like his;" and the declaration of the revelator, "Blessed are the dead that die in the Lord from henceforth; yea, saith the Spirit, that they may rest from their labors; and their works do follow them;" and the promise of God himself concerning his faithful servant, "With long life

will I satisfy him and show him my salvation ;"—
as I remembered these things, I felt a new inspi-
ration to come to you and wish and pray that
your Christmas might be glad with the joy of
every sweet domestic affection, with every out-
pouring of good will to man and glory to God
in the highest, with every grace from him whose
name is called Emmanuel.

I must speak of that of which my heart is full.
May you all find God with you, as he for whom
we mourn lived close to his Saviour and his
God, and may you also, if God so will, live out
in peace the days of man and go from earth in
the fullness of years as he has gone, fulfilling the
aspiration of his own evening hymn :

" How sweet to look in thoughtful hope
  Beyond this fading sky,
And hear him call his children up
  To his fair home on high.

" Calmly the day forsakes our heaven
  To dawn beyond the west ;
So may my soul in life's last even
  Retire to glorious rest."